# Homemade Melt and Pour Soaps
## Instruction To Make Soaps At Home

Copyright © 2020

### DEDICATION

# Contents

# The Basics of Melt and Pour Soap Making

### Choosing a Soap Base

The process of making any melt and pour soap begins with choosing a base.

There are a number of different options to choose from. But it is important to understand that not all soap bases are as eco-friendly and natural as you might wish. Some of the most sustainable, natural options are:

- Goats milk soap base.

- Honey soap base.
- Shea butter soap base.
- Oatmeal soap base.
- Natural glycerin soap base.

Once you have decided on a base, you need to decide what you would like to add to the base to create a soap that works well and looks great.

**Additions for Your Melt and Pour Soap**

For example, you might want to add:

- Natural Exfoliants – such as salt, oats, coffee etc..
- Herbs and botanicals – for their natural, healthy properties and their appearance.
- Essential oils – for their scent, and beneficial properties.
- Natural pigments or dyes – such as natural clays, minerals, herbs and spices, vegetable-based dyes etc..

There are a wide range of natural additions you can make to create the perfect soaps for your needs.

You could also consider making two-in-one soaps and cleaners, by placing a piece of natural loofah or natural sponge into your melt and pour soap creations.

**Molds for Your Simple Soaps**

You will also need to buy or make some molds to shape your soaps. There are a great many different options out there to choose from.

You could simply use kitchen items like muffin trays to make your own soaps without having to invest in molds specifically for the purpose.

You could also make your own molds by cutting a milk or juice carton in half, or making your own wooden soap mold, then slicing soap bars from the larger block you create.

If you want round soaps, one simple hack is to use lengths of upcycled plumbing piping as molds.

Of course, you could also choose to buy a wooden, or silicone soap mold.

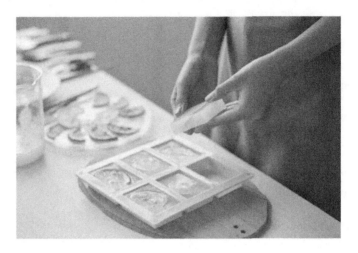

Silicone soap molds allow you to ring the changes and make soaps in a much wider range of shapes and sizes. For example, you can find honeycomb and bee molds, insect molds, heart-shaped molds, flower molds, and many, many more.

You do not have to restrict yourself to merely making soaps in simple, geometric shapes.

Melt and pour recipes are a great way to get started with soap making.

Even children could help you make soap in this way. So it could be a fun activity to enjoy with the whole family.

There is quite a lot of leeway in this activity. Therefore, it is quite easy to experiment, and to develop recipes that work for you.

# Milk and Honey Melt and Pour Soap

Both goats milk and honey have excellent properties that make them perfect for use on your skin.

This simplest of melt and pour soap making recipes involves combining a goat's milk soap base with pure, natural organic honey. It can be made in just ten minutes or so, and is naturally moisturising, clarifying, soothing and antibacterial.

Prep Time: 5 minutes

Cook Time: 5 minutes

**Ingredients**

2 lb Goat Milk Soap Base

5 tbsp Raw Honey

Gold Soap Colorant

91% Isopropyl Alcohol, in a spray bottle

Microwave-safe Measuring Cup

12" Silicone Honeycomb Mold

**Directions**

1. Slice the goat's milk soap base into small cubes and place into a microwave-safe measuring cup. Melt in the microwave in 30-second increments, stirring well after each session, to ensure that the soap is completely melted.
2. Carefully stir in gold soap colorant and honey. Pour the melted soap into the mold and spritz with isopropyl alcohol to remove any air bubbles.

3. Allow the soaps to sit undisturbed until completely firm (approximately 60-90 minutes depending on temperature and humidity) before unmolding.

# Goat's Milk and Himalayan Salt Soap

This is another easy recipe. It combines a goat's milk soap base with organic jojoba oil or organic almond oil, Himalayan salts for exfoliation, and essential oils of your choice. (Sweet orange and frankincense are suggested, though many other essential oils can also work well.)

Prep Time:15 minutes

Cook Time:5 minutes

Total Time:20 minutes

**Ingredients**

2 cups of melt and pour organic soap base with goat milk cut them in cubes so they can melt

faster

a double boileror an aluminium bowl placed into a pan of water

3 tablespoons of organic jojoba oil or organic almond oil

Himalayan salts

20 drops of Sweet orange 5 drops of all spice eo and 10 drops of frankincense essential oils (or any essential oils of your choice - total max 30 drops)

**Directions**

1. Cut the melt and pour soap base into small cubes so they melt faster
2. Add them to your double boiler on low to medium heat (basically a aluminium recipient in a pan of warm water)
3. Continue steering until the soap base is melted
4. Once melted, add the jojoba or almond oil, mix well. You could also substitute with any carrier oil of your choice.
5. Add essential oils if desired, mix well.
6. Put a little bit of Himalayan salts at the bottom of the mold
7. Pour in the silicone mold.
8. Spray pure alcohol on top of the soap to get rid of the bubbles if any
9. Add the Himalayan salt on top of the soaps while the soap is still liquid
10. Let dry for 24h hours before un-molding. Voila, its ready to use!

# Lavender and Rosemary Soap

This simple melt and pour soap also uses a goat's milk base. It enriches that base with rosemary and lavender, in both dried and essential oil form.

Lavender and rosemary both smell great, and also offer a range of health and cosmetic benefits.

Lavender is relaxing. It is also a powerful antiseptic which can kill a range of common bacteria. What is more, it can be soothing, and help prevent the formation of permanent scar tissue. Rosemary can help stimulate blood flow and help circulation, and is a herb often used as a stimulant in aromatherapy.

**Ingredients**:

1/2 lb. goat's milk soap base

2 tablespoons dried rosemary

2 tablespoons dried lavender

10 drops rosemary essential oil

10 drops lavender essential oil

Soap coloring (optional)

Soap mold

Spritz bottle filled with rubbing alcohol

**Directions**

1. COLOR PREP: Dispersing powders in alcohol helps them mix into the melt and pour soap without clumps. Mix 4 teaspoons of rose clay with 1 tablespoon of 99% isopropyl alcohol and 2 teaspoons of rosehip powder with 1 tablespoon of 99% isopropyl alcohol. The exact amount of alcohol is not extremely important – add more if necessary to create a thick paste. Set colorants aside. Pour alcohol in the spray bottle and set aside.

2. Chop 32 ounces of White Melt and Pour Soap Base into small uniform pieces. Place all the soap into a large heat-safe bowl. Place the bowl into the microwave and melt the soap using 30 second bursts. Between each burst, stir the soap to help it melt evenly and prevent overheating. Continue heating and stirring until the base is

completely melted.

3. Add all of the dispersed rose clay and rosehip powder to the melted soap and stir to fully mix in the powders.

4. Add 0.3 oz. of lavender 40/42 essential oil, 0.3 oz. of lemongrass essential oil, and 2 Tbsp. of poppy seeds. Stir to fully mix in the ingredients.

5. Once the soap is poured into the mold, the mold shouldn't be moved or the seal could break. Move the mold to where you'd like it to fully cool and harden. Check the temperature of the soap. If it's above 130° F, the poppy seeds may fall to the bottom of the mold. Once the soap is about 125° F, carefully pour into the mold. Use one hand to steady the mold as you pour to prevent it from falling over.

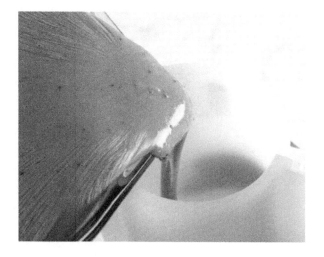

6. Spritz the top with 99% isopropyl alcohol to get rid of bubbles. Allow the soap to fully cool and harden for at least 4 hours or up to overnight.

7. Once the soap is completely cool and hard, remove from the mold. Use a crinkle cutter to cut the soap into bars. Cut them as thin or as thick as you'd like. You can use a non-serrated knife if you prefer a smooth look. Wrap the soap in plastic wrap to prevent glycerin dew and enjoy.

# Organic Peppercorn Massage Melt and Pour Soap

The whole black peppercorns in this soap recipe naturally massage the skin and promote good circulation whenever the soap is used. Meanwhile, orange zest adds little pops of colour, as well as a hint of fragrance. The soap uses a glycerin base, and suggests a combination of clove, basil and lavender essential oils.

**Ingredients:**

12.5 oz. organic melt and pour glycerin soap base

.25 oz. orange zest

.5 oz. organic whole black peppercorns

10 drops organic clove essential oil

10 drops organic basil essential oil

10 drops organic lavender essential oil

**Directions:**

1. I used a square Gladware container as my mold for this melt and pour soap recipe and lined it with a plastic office trash bag. I used masking tape to hold the lining in place. You could also use plastic cling film to line your mold. Once your mold is ready, weight out 12.5 oz. of my glycerin soap base using a digital scale, cut it into chunks and then place it inside a large glass Pyrex measuring cup. Melt the soap base in the microwave on reduced power and remove once melted.

2. Now weigh out your peppercorns and orange zest – I cut my zest from the rind of fresh orange – and stir into your melted soap base. Using a different plastic transfer pipette or glass dropper for each essential oil, add ten drops of each essential oil to the soap mixture and stir well to blend.

3. Now pour your liquid soap base into your lined mold. You can spritz the top of your soap lightly with witch hazel or alcohol to get rid of any air bubbles on the top of the soap. Your additives will settle to the bottom and top of the soap. (If you'd like the peppercorns and orange zest to distribute evenly throughout the entire bar, use a suspension melt and pour glycerin soap base.) Next, place your filled mold in the freezer until your soap has hardened completely.

4. Once your soap has solidified, remove from the mold and cut into bars. Finally wrap tightly in plastic wrap until ready to use.

# Turmeric Melt & Pour Soap

Turmeric imparts a lovely warm yellow hue to your soap. But it has practical benefits too.

This member of the ginger family contains curcumin. This is an antioxidant which is believed to have anti-inflammatory properties. Turmeric also acts as a natural anti-bacterial.

The simple recipe below combines turmeric with a goat's milk soap base and orange essential oil. But you could also consider adding other ingredients – fresh ginger, for example, might be a good fit.

### Ingredients

12 Cavity Rectangle Silicone Mold

60 oz. Goat Milk Melt and Pour Soap Base

2 tsp. Turmeric Powder

0.8 oz. Orange 10X Essential Oil

2 Tbsp. 99% Isopropyl Alcohol in Spray Bottle

### Directions

1. Chop 60 ounces of Goat Milk Melt and Pour Soap Base into small, uniform cubes. Place the soap into a large, heat-safe container and melt in the microwave using 60-second bursts. Because it's such a large amount of soap, it will take a little longer to melt.

2. While the soap is in the microwave, mix 2 teaspoons of turmeric powder with 2 tablespoons of 99% isopropyl alcohol. Doing so helps the turmeric more easily mix into the melted soap without chunks.

3. In a glass, essential oil-safe container, measure 0.8 ounces of Orange 10X Essential Oil.

4. Once the soap is melted, add all the dispersed turmeric powder and the Orange 10X Essential Oil. Use a spatula to mix the ingredients thoroughly.

5.  Pour the soap into each cavity of the mold. After each pour, spray the top of the bars with 99% isopropyl alcohol to help get rid of bubbles. Allow the soap to fully cool and harden. Remove from the mold and enjoy! Wrap the soap in plastic wrap after unmolding to prevent glycerin dew.

# Coffee Soap

Who doesn't love the scent of fresh-brewed coffee? This simple melt and pour soap recipe uses coffee both for its fragrance and for its natural exfoliating property.

Caffeine is also a useful anti-inflammatory for the skin, and can make skin less puffy, improve circulation and reduce water retention.

**Ingredients**

1 pound goats milk melt and pour soap base , shea butter soap base would be OK too

1/4 cup coffee grounds

1/4 tsp vanilla essential oil (Oleoresin) or coffee fragrance oil ***optional***

large cube silicone mold (or make double batch in loaf mold)

**Directions**

1. Cut soap into smaller pieces. Place in microwave safe bowl along with coffee grounds. Microwave for 40 seconds, stir then repeat in 10-20 second intervals until soap in fully melted.
2. Remove and stir until soap begins to slightly slightly thicken (add fragrance if you wish at this point and stir in). Pour into the soap mold and allow to cool fully.
3. Cut into slices to create bars.

**Notes**

Time: Takes about 10 minutes to make, but then must cool at least an hour (or more) before cutting.

**Benefits Of Coffee Soap**

Coffee soap benefits are numerous. Here is why adding a coffee bar of soap to your skin care routine is worth it.

First of all the coffee grounds of course have a mild exfoliating effect. Sloughing of old dead skin is always a good thing for ensuring a fresh look.

Caffeine is anti-inflammatory for the skin.

Reduces water retention, making skin look less puffy and improves circulation (both are good for reducing the appearance of cellulite).

# Herb + Spice Homemade Glycerin Soap

Suspend dried herbs, flowers, and spices in a clear glycerin soap base and add essential oils for a customized pampering treat. These decorative soaps also look beautiful when displayed in your bathroom.

**Ingredients**

Dried flowers and/or leaves Rosemary, eucalyptus, hibiscus, juniper berries, dried citrus peels

Glycerin melt and pour soap

Essential oils - eucalyptus, lemon, rosemary, orange, etc.

Molds - cups or trays in various sizes silicone works best

**Directions**

1. Cut the glycerin soap into pieces. Melt according to package directions.
2. Carefully and slowly add the essential oils, about 5 drops per ounce of soap used. Stir gently and slowly to prevent bubbles from forming. Gently rap the jar or container on the countertop to release any larger trapped air bubbles.

3. Place the dried flowers or herbs into the mold and carefully fill each one with the melted soap base.

4. Let cool completely, about 1 hour. Pop out of the molds and store in an airtight container or package to give as a gift.

# White Tea & Ginger Loofah Soap

**Ingredients:**

30 oz. clear detergent free glycerin melt & pour soap base

.9 oz. White Tea & Ginger Fragrance Oil, of choice

20 drops orange liquid soap colorant

5 inch Luffa

Tools & Equipment:

Crafters Choice™ Basic Round Silicone Soap Mold

digital scale

bread knife

Chef's knife

large Pyrex measuring cup

utensil (for stirring)

spray bottle with alcohol

microwave

**Directions**

1.  Begin by using a bread knife to cut your loofah into slices approximately 1" thick.

2. Place the loofah slices into each of the six cavities of your mold.

3. Now cut your soap base into square chunks using a Chef's knife. Weigh out 30 oz. of soap and place in a large Pyrex measuring cup. Melt in the microwave just until all

40

the soap has melted. Watch your soap carefully as it will bubble up and overflow if it gets too hot.

4. Weigh out the fragrance oil and stir into the melted soap base. Add 20 drops of the liquid melt and pour soap colorant and mix well.

5. Now pour the scented and colored soap base into each of the cavities of your mold. As the loofah absorbs some of the soap you'll be able to go back and fill each cavity completely.

6. Allow the soap base to set up and harden completely, then carefully push each loofah soap out of the mold.

# Activated Charcoal Soap

Combine shea butter soap base, activated charcoal, and tea tree essential oil for a soap that's perfect for acne prone skin.

**Ingredients**

1/2 pound shea butter soap base

5 activated charcoal capsules (if you can't find at a pharmacy you can buy it online or use 1 teaspoon of loose powder)

15-20 drops tea tree essential oil

charcoal soap-6

**Directions**

1. Cut the soap base into small chunks and place in a microwave safe bowl. Heat in 30-second intervals until completely melted. (You can also use a double boiler to melt the soap, if you prefer.)

2. Remove a small amount of soap into a cup and let cool slightly. Open the charcoal capsules and mix charcoal into slightly cooled soap until blended and no lumps remain. Add back into the rest of the melted soap base and stir well to fully disperse charcoal.

3. Add the tea tree oil. If you don't like the smell of tea tree, you can add peppermint essential oil to hide the scent.

4. Pour into mold (I have used silicon baking molds and muffin tins as molds — both work well) and let cool completely before removing.

5.

**Some helpful tips:**

Adding charcoal to a small portion of soap should help it mix better. If you're having problems with clumping, use a wire whisk to break them up.

Only when you've gotten rid of all clumps should you add it to the larger portion of soap base.

Feel free to lightly coat your muffin tin with nonstick spray if you're worried about your soaps sticking. Otherwise, just put the muffin tin in the freezer for 5-10 minutes and they should pop right out.

These soaps should last about 6 months.

# Exfoliating Coffee and Cinnamon Soap

**Ingredients**:

Makes about 25 bars.

1.5 litres olive oil

175 grams lye

350 grams water

1-5 tablespoons ground coffee

20 or so drops cinnamon essential oil

A little cinnamon to sprinkle over the top of the soap to make it look cool, if you like

**Directions**

1. To make the soap base, follow my homemade Castile soap recipe here, pausing when the soap reaches the trace stage. That's the time to add the ground coffee and cinnamon essential oil.

2. Adding more ground coffee will make the soap a richer brown colour and also up its exfoliating properties. Add cinnamon oil until you can smell it in the mixture. Keep in mind that the scent will dull as the soap dries and cures.

3. Mix well and fold the soap into a mould. Cure and cut according to the base recipe instructions.

4. Your beautifully scented, exfoliating soap should be ready to use within a couple weeks.

# Rosemary Lemon Kitchen Soap

**Ingredients**

1 pound melt and pour soap

4 teaspoons grapeseed oil

1 teaspoon lemon essential oil

1 teaspoon dried rosemary

Pyrex glass measuring cup

Soap mold

**Directions**

1. Cut melt and pour soap in to small chunks. Melt in the microwave at 30 second intervals until melted. Stir between intervals.

2. Add grapeseed oil and stir.

3. Let cool until it just starts to thicken. Add dried rosemary.

4. Add lemon essential oil.

5. Add a drop of yellow food coloring if desired.

6. Let sit until the top just starts to get a film on it. Pour into the mold and let sit until cool.

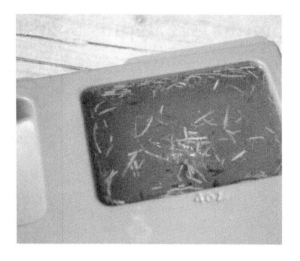

7. This smells amazing!

# Grapefruit Eucalyptus Soap Bars

Melt & Pour soap can be a lot of fun. As far as soap making methods go, this one probably offers the widest range of complexity. You can keep things easy by making a solid colored soap, or spice things up with layers, additives, and embedding. It all just depends on how much you feel like taking on.

**Ingredients**

1 pound Clear Coconut Melt & Pour Base

2 tablespoons White Kaolin Clay

1 tablespoon Aloe Vera Gel (or water)

2 teaspoons Avocado Oil, divided

1/2 teaspoon Jeweltone Garnet Mica

1/2 teaspoon Jeweltone Emerald Mica

1 – 2 teaspoons Enchanted Eucalypus Plant-Based Fragrance Oil

1 – 2 teaspoons Grapefruit Splash Plant-Based Fragrance Oil

A small sprayer bottle filled with rubbing alcohol

**Directions**

1. Cut the Melt & Pour Base into cubes, then melt it in a double boiler.
2. Mix the Kaolin Clay and Aloe Vera Gel together in a small bowl, then mix that paste into the soap base.
3. In two other bowls, mix each of the micas with 1 teaspoon of Avocado Oil, forming a slurry in each bowl.
4. Remove the soap base from the heat, and divide it in half. Add the Gemtone Emerald Mica and Enchanted Eucalyptus Plant-Based Fragrance Oil to the first half, mixing well to thoroughly combine the ingredients. Return the second half of the base to the heat so that it remains melted.
5. Carefully pour the colored and scented soap into your soap molds, filling each mold about halfway up. Allow the soap to cool and harden until the top layer of the soap

sets.

6. Once the first half of the soap sets just enough to support the second layer, start working on your second half of the soap. Remove it from the heat, and mix in the Gemtone Garnet Mica and the Grapefruit Splash Plant-Based Fragrance Oil. Mix the ingredients well to combine.

7. Spritz each soap in the mold with rubbing alcohol, then carefully pour the second layer of soap into the molds. Allow the bars to cool and harden completely before removing them from the mold.

# Gemstone Soaps

Each kit includes (makes a minimum of 2 soaps):

1/2lb each of vegetable based clear and opaque white soap bases

red, yellow, green and blue food coloring

10 small, reusable mixing cups

2 soap molds

toothpicks

**Ingredients**

a microwavable glass or measuring cup

paring knife

cutting board

scissors

fragrance oil (optional)

**Directions**

1. Start by cutting each of your soap bases in half. Reserve the clear and opaque halves for your 2nd gemstone soap – the kit will allow you to make a minimum of 2 soaps in 2 color ways. Cut the halves in half again. One quarter piece of the clear and opaque soap will be used mix colors. The other quarters pieces will be reserved for the final mold.

2. Cut the clear soap into small chunks and place into a microwavable glass. Microwave for 40-60 seconds until completely melted. If you want to add fragrance, this is when you'd add your oil. A little goes a long way so don't overdo it! Divide the melted soap evenly into 5 small mixing cups.

3. I'll be making purple here which means I'll need to mix blue and red. Start with the darkest shades first. One drop of each color should really be as dark as you'll need to go. Slowly reduce the amount of food coloring after each subsequent mixing cup. Use the toothpick to extract the smallest amount of color from the bottle. Again, a little goes a long way! Mix each color thoroughly with a toothpick. If the soap starts to set, then pop them mini cups into the microwave for 4-5 seconds and mix again.

Color combination tips:

red + blue = purple

red + yellow = orange

blue + green = cyan

green + yellow + red = brown

4. Repeat the same step with the quarter pound of opaque soap base. Allow to set for at least an hour or so. Once they've cooled and hardened, turn them over, use your thumbs to push the bottom and they should pop out easily. Save the mini mixing cups as you'll be able to reuse them over and over again.

61

5. Slice the colors into thin slices and small shards. Mix the colors randomly and drop them into the soap mold. The looser and more random, the better. I like to place the darker colors on the bottom and lighter colors on top but again, don't try to get it too uniform!

6. Melt the quarter piece of clear soap and pour into the soap mold. Then melt the quarter piece of opaque soap and pour into the soap mold.

7. At this point, you can even pop the entire cup into the microwave for 5 seconds – just so the colors melt together more naturally. Or you can leave it as it is. The cup might warp from the hot soap – it's okay. Just keep an eye on it if you do decide to put it in the microwave – you don't want to melt a hole in your mold! Allow to set for a couple of hours – you can even pop it in the refrigerator if you, like me, don't have the patience to wait. Once the soap has totally cooled and hardened, carefully cut the mold open with a pair of scissors.

8. Place the wider end on a cutting board and use a paring knife to cut 5-6 vertical edges at a slight angle. Then cut the top into a point at 5-6 more exaggerated angles.

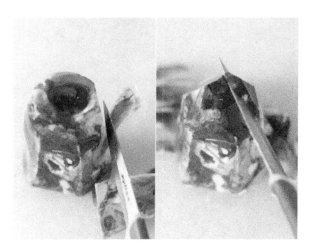

9. And voila, that's it!

# Confetti Soap

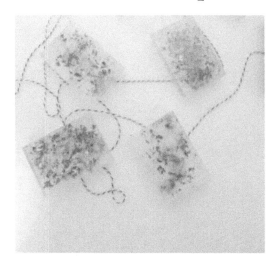

**Ingredients**:

rectangle soap mold

melt and pour clear glycerin soap

confetti

vegetable spray

fragrance

paper, etc. for wrapping

**Directions**

1. Prepare your mold by spraying with vegetable spray. This will help the soap come out easily once set. Cut your soap into squares, and place into a glass, microwave-safe bowl. Microwave according to package instructions.

2. Once soap is melted (be careful not to overheat, as this can affect the consistency of the soap), add fragrance. I used doTERRA Wild Orange Essential Oil, and added 6 or so drops to the soap mixture. Mix well, and then pour into molds.

3. After pouring soap into molds, add a pinch of confetti to each mold, and stir in using a wooden dowel. You will need to work quickly, as the soap sets faster than you'd think!

4. Put in the refrigerator, and let set for 30 minutes, or until hard. Gently pop out soap once set. Having a hard time getting the soap out? Just put the mold in the freezer for a couple of minutes!

5. The fun begins! Wrap and decorate your soap with whatever materials you choose. I chose scrapbook paper, twine and washi tape, but there are so many creative ways to make your soap gift-worthy!

Made in the USA
Las Vegas, NV
07 December 2024

13443430R00049